Exploring Andalusia

by Julia Begbie and Calum Chace

Contents

For Alex

EXPLORING ANDALUSIA

A Three Cs book
ISBN 978-1-8383668-2-7

Acknowledgements
Calum and Julia would like to thank the following for their comments and suggestions, while at the same time absolving them of blame for any mistakes in the finished product:
Luis Rey.
Patrick Elvin, Clare Copeman, and Michael Barry.
Turespana, the Spanish Tourist office in London.
Anne Razvi, Rosa de Lima Orellana Sanchez, Jo Hepplewhite, Matthew Wolfmann, Jacqueline Cockburn, Ira Goldberg, David Charlton, Howard Eames, Freda Collinson, Lynne Morison.

Other books by Calum Chace
The Economic Singularity (3rd edition)
Surviving AI (3rd edition)
Pandora's Oracle
Pandora's Brain
Stories From 2045 (editor and contributor)
Artificial Intelligence and the Two Singularities
Our Jobless Future
The Internet Startup Bible (co-author)
The Internet Consumer Bible (co-author)

Introduction to Andalusia

Since you're reading this book, you probably already know that Andalusia has a great deal more to offer than beaches and hotel pools. But it seems you are in a minority. Spain is the second most-visited country in the world after France, but the great majority of Andalusia's visitors head straight for the beaches and stay there. Tourism comprises 10% of Spanish GDP, but apart from Barcelona, most of it is spent on the Costas, in the Balearics, and in the Canaries.

Given where the visitors come from, this is understandable: the biggest source of visitors is Britain, a country in need of a roof, and vitamin D on tap. The Costa del Sol receives twice as much sun as the UK, and just two-thirds the amount of rain –and while it is not true that the rain in Spain falls mainly on the plain, it is true that it falls mainly in concentrated downpours, not in long days of drizzle.

However understandable their behaviour, those visitors basking on the Costas are missing a great deal. Spain has more UNESCO World Heritage sites than any other country except for Italy and China – 48 at the time of writing. Of those 48 sites, eight are in Andalusia, which is one-third as many as the whole of the United States.

Away from the coast, Andalusia offers spectacular unspoilt mountain landscapes, with some of the best hiking country anywhere in the world. Startling glossy green pines seem to spark electricity against the ultramarine blue sky. The endless forests of cork oaks, chestnut and eucalyptus trees cloak the long valleys that sweep down towards the Mediterranean, providing welcome cool by oleander-fringed river pools. In spring especially, the colour palette of flowers is quite literally breath-taking. The area is famous for the diversity of both migratory and local bird populations, and looking down from a mountain top as vultures and eagles soar below should be on everyone's bucket list.

Andalusia's built environment is no less special. It has more than its fair share of pre-history, including dolmens (megalithic table-like structures) at Antequerra and cave paintings at Cueva de la Pileta. The Roman amphitheatre at Italica is second only to the Colosseum in Rome, and it has other well-preserved Roman sites at Bolonia and Acinipo.

Its white villages are world-famous for the simple beauty of their white-washed walls and tiled roofs, and their infectiously laconic lifestyle. There are dozens to explore, each with its own particular charm, most of them arrayed around a church and a castle.

Spain was once a great colonial power, and parts of Andalusia luxuriate quietly in the trappings of empire. But Andalusia also has something completely unique: the architectural gems of al-Andalus. The 800-year period when Muslims ruled southern Spain created a culture with roots in north African and Arabian traditions, but blended with European influences to create something new, sublime, and unavailable anywhere else.

Last but certainly not least, Andalusia has fertile soil, a very particular agricultural heritage, and a rich culinary culture that combines the healthy and delicious Mediterranean diet with its own native crops and north African flavours. Spain's most famous wine region is Rioja, in the north, but Andalusia is home to a number of excellent wine-makers, especially in Granada and Lebrija, and of course it is the home of sherry, one of the world's most highly-regarded fortified wines.

Cities and towns

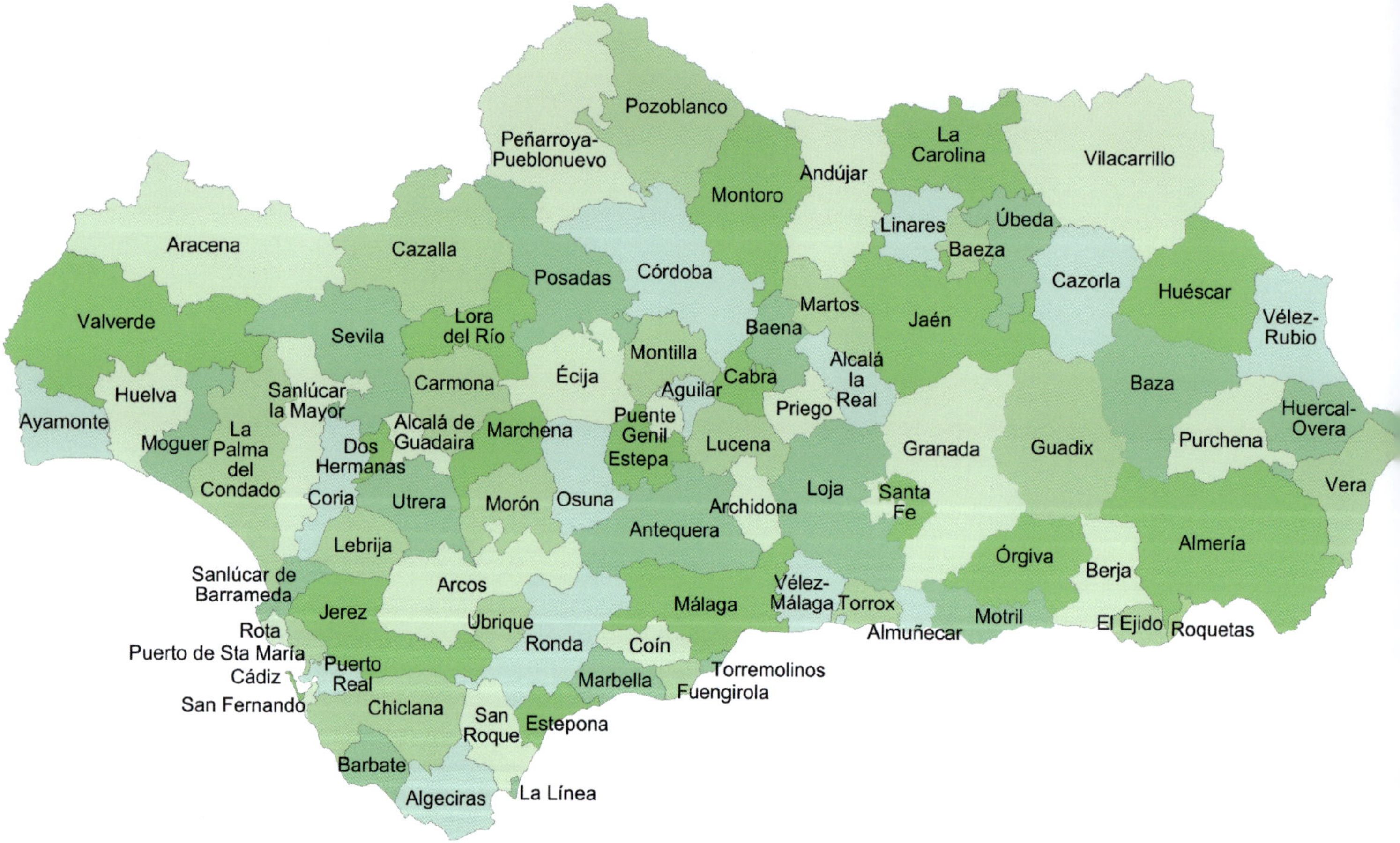
Pozoblanco
Peñarroya-
Pueblonuevo
Montoro
Andújar
La
Carolina
Vilacarrillo
Linares
Úbeda
Baeza
Aracena
Cazalla
Posadas
Córdoba
Cazorla
Huéscar
Valverde
Sevila
Lora
del Río
Martos
Baena
Jaén
Vélez-
Rubio
Montilla
Alcalá
la
Real
Écija
Carmona
Cabra
Aguilar
Huelva
Sanlúcar
la Mayor
Baza
Ayamonte
Moguer
La
Palma
del
Condado
Alcalá de
Guadaira
Marchena
Puente
Genil
Estepa
Priego
Lucena
Granada
Guadix
Purchena
Huercal-
Overa
Dos
Hermanas
Coria
Utrera
Morón
Osuna
Archidona
Loja
Santa
Fe
Vera
Antequera
Lebrija
Almería
Órgiva
Berja
Sanlúcar de
Barrameda
Arcos
Vélez-
Málaga
Torrox
Málaga
Jerez
Motril
Almuñecar
El Ejido
Roquetas
Ubrique
Rota
Ronda
Coín
Puerto de Sta María
Puerto
Real
Cádiz
Torremolinos
Marbella
Fuengirola
San Fernando
Chiclana
San
Roque
Estepona
Barbate
Algeciras
La Línea

The Grand Tour of Andalusia

In the late 17th century, young British aristocrats and gentry began to travel soauth through France and Switzerland to Italy – partly to complete their education, partly as a rite of passage. The itinerary was fairly consistent, featuring Paris, Geneva, Florence, Venice, Rome and Naples. A few went on to Greece, and many returned to Britain via Vienna, Berlin and Munich. The trip was usually taken with a knowledgeable guide, who was also expected to act as chaperone, and could take a few months or even years.

The great value of the Grand Tour was supposed to be familiarisation with the art and culture of the classical civilisations of Greece and Rome, although many of the young men, being young men, seemed to take a more particular interest in the liberal mores of the local young women.

The ritual of the Grand Tour petered out as the age of mass travel arrived, thanks to rail and steam ships, but it left a legacy: many Brits still think of Italy as the essential destination for cultural tourism. And with good reason: the glory of Rome and the marvels of the Renaissance have a strong claim on our intellectual imaginations, and there is much to admire about the Italian determination to live stylishly and live well. It takes a wooden heart to be unmoved by a visit to Florence or Venice.

Very few of these wealthy tourists turned west to visit Spain, which is a pity. Andalusia cannot rival the great Italian cities for paintings (you have to go to Madrid and Barcelona for that), but its architecture, its landscapes, and its culinary culture are second to none.

Spain was an important Roman province, and Andalusia exhibits that legacy at Bologna near Tarifa, Acinipo near Ronda, and Italica near Seville. As the great colonial power of Central and South America, Spain acquired huge wealth and the cultural trappings that go with it. This wealth entered Spain through ports in Andalusia, and although much of it was transferred to the royal power centre in Madrid, it certainly left its mark down south.

And of course Andalusia has something unique: the stunning architectural achievements of Al-Andalus. These jewels comprise what we like to think of as Andalusia's grand tour.

The eight centuries of Muslim rule in Spain make a fascinating historical saga. It starts with the tragi-comic (and probably fictional) story of a Vandal noble who, outraged by his king's lewd behaviour towards his daughter, summoned a foreign army from across the Mediterranean to obtain vengeance, only to find his whole civilisation being swept aside by that army. It continues with a complex tapestry of competing and interlacing tribes and rivalries, alliances and conquests, enough to fill a thousand historical novels.

The city of **Cordoba**, with its unique and entrancing combination of mosque and cathedral, was the seat of al-Andalus' finest era, when Muslims, Christians and Jews worked in harmony to produce a culture whose arts and sciences led the world. Cordoba surpassed Constantinople to become the biggest city in Europe.

After the fall of the caliphate of Cordoba in 1031, al-Andalus fragmented into mini-kingdoms (taifas), but was re-united under two more waves of invaders from north Africa, the veiled Almoravids and the even more extreme Almohads. **Seville** became their capital, but its architectural jewels (like the magnificent Alcazar palace) are mostly in the Mudejar style, which was developed from Islamic traditions by Christian craftsmen for Christian patrons. Later, in the sixteenth century, Seville held a monopoly over trade with Spain's colonies in the Americas, which gave it a century-long "golden age".

Granada's Alhambra palace complex is the high point of al-Andalus art and architecture, although the Nasrid dynasty which built it was a relatively minor power, beset by violent intrigue, and presiding over the decline and fall of Muslim Spain.

The Alhambra deserves its reputation for architectural excellence: there is a very good reason why you have to book a visit months in advance.

Finally, there is **Malaga**. Overlooked by many people as simply the location of Andalusia's main airport, and the gateway to the Costa del Sol, it was never a capital of al-Andalus, unlike the other three stops on our Grand Tour. But it is second in population only to Seville, and it boasts so many treasures from all periods of Spain's colourful history that it is sometimes called an open-air museum. The Alcazaba fortress and palace complex bears comparison to its peers in Seville and Granada, and its cathedral is, to coin a phrase, full-on Ridley Scott. And odd as this may sound, its car museum is not to be missed.

Granada

Sometimes, architecture can make your spirit soar. Sometimes, when you enter a room or a courtyard, a combination of great craftsmanship and harmonious design can take your breath away at the same time as it makes your heart sing. Sometimes, a building is just about perfect – almost transcendent. Granada's Alhambra is such a place.

It shouldn't be, really. The Nasrid rulers who built it were a nasty bunch. Most of them seized power by assassinating a family member and lost it the same way. Their empire was not so much the final flowering of Moorish culture as its fag end.

They hung onto their corner of Spain for fully two centuries after the rest of Al-Andalus had fallen to the Christians partly because its mountainous terrain was hard to conquer, but more because of bribery: they made regular payments to the Christian kingdom of Castile. The Christians were also preoccupied with fighting among themselves. Once they managed to unite, it was only a matter of time before Granada fell.

The Nasrids didn't sponsor much innovation in art or architecture, and some commentators have suggested that they cheated by decorating their interiors with stucco rather than marble and carved stone. But this is unreasonable: they created a jewel by synthesising much of what had gone before, employing Moorish craftsmen who had few other places to work.

At its height, in 719AD, Al-Andalus contained almost the whole of what we now call Spain, and their territory reached over the Pyrenees into France beyond Carcassonne. Five hundred years later, when Ibn Nasr established the emirate of Granada in 1230, the only other part of Spain controlled by the Moors was Cordoba, which was just about to fall to the Christians.

The Alhambra's name comes from the Arabic phrase "al-hamra", the red one. Both the Spanish and the English give it another definite article, so strictly speaking, we are calling it "the the red one." The Spanish never pronounce the letter "h", but they don't mind at all when we do.

The Alhambra is a UNESCO World Heritage Site, and was one of the 20 finalists of the global competition to choose the seven new wonders of the world on the seventh day of the seventh month of 2007.

It is Spain's most-visited site (Barcelona's Sagrada Familia comes second), with 2.5 million tickets sold in normal years. So when you go, make sure to book well in advance! Visits are timed, and ever-so-slightly regimented: no going backwards, no sitting down, no leaning on walls. But this is not a complaint. The crowd control is unobtrusive, and you are afforded plenty of time to enjoy the sights. Most people spend around three hours at the site, and in the summer it pays to go early to beat the heat.

Running from west to east (right to left), the Alhambra consists of three parts: an "alcazaba" (a fortress), an "alcázar" (a palace, for the emir) and the "medina" (a small city for courtiers and officials).

They were constructed with a mix of stone aggregate and red clay, which is where the name comes from, although the red colour is only obvious at dusk.

Although the Alhambra's name comes from its exterior, its fame derives from its decorated interiors. The first highlight of the palace is the court of the Myrtles, overlooked by the Hall of the Ambassadors. Its name comes from the myrtle bushes that surround the 34-metre long central pond.

Then comes the famous court of the lions. First-time visitors are often taken aback by the frankly risible appearance of the lions, but the rest of the space is so sublime that you quickly forget that the stone animals holding the fountain at its centre look more like overgrown pussycats than fierce predators. Representation of living beings are rare in Islamic art, and these lions suggest the sculptors could have done with a lot more practice.

One of the stunning reception areas illustrates the gory reality of Nasrid rule. The hall of the Abencerrajes is named after a noble family which the emir had slaughtered en masse because, the story goes, one of them was caught climbing up a wall towards the window of a royal lady. This long-ago tragedy fades as you look upwards to the halls' ceiling.

The room is square, with graceful columns support soaring arches decorated in blue, red, and gold, culminating in an eight-pointed star-shaped cupola. All over the ceiling are the characteristic stalactite formation of honeycombed cells, almost fractal in their complexity.

Throughout the palace, the decoration is divided into two by a ceramic dado rail. Above is a profusion of stucco carvings of Islamic scripts, so complex, interwoven, and illustrative that it looks like foliage. The text is mostly verses from the Qu'ran and poems composed by members of the Nasrid court.

Below the dado are glazed tiles with geometric patterns. These may look less complex, but in fact the Alhambra is said to be the only place in the world where you can find all the 17 possible types of patterns which mathematicians call symmetry groups – or more prosaically, wallpaper groups.

Leaving the Alhambra uphill and to the east, you can visit the Generalife, a separate summer residence for the court.

Its gardens and pools are charming, although to our mind excelled by the gardens of the Alcazar in Seville.

The Generalife is one of the oldest Moorish gardens in the world, but it was extensively re-designed and re-planted, first in the 16th century, and again in the 20th century.

Its numerous courtyards and palace buildings bear names appropriate for discussions of affairs of state and affairs of the heart, like the courtyard of the sultana, and the walk of the oleanders.

Back in the Alhambra complex itself, you'll find the dramatically discordant Carlos V palace. Granada fell to the Christians in 1492, at the hands of Isabella and Ferdinand, whose marriage united the kingdoms of Aragon and Castille.

Their grandson, Carlos V, wanted to make the Alhambra his base, but found its accommodation cold and gloomy, so he decided to build a new palace where he could live with the woman he had, unexpectedly, fallen in love with prior to their marriage.

Thankfully he decided against knocking down significant elements of the Nasrid site, but the building he commissioned was neo-classical renaissance in style, and completely at odds with its surroundings.

It is, however, an intriguing building in its own right, with an innovative circular patio occupying the whole interior. Carlos and his queen never lived there, as he spent the rest of his life touring Europe, defending Catholicism from the invading Turks, and then from Protestantism.

The Alhambra fell into disrepair and was occupied by squatters. It was rediscovered, not least by itinerant Brits, after the expulsion of Napoleon in what they called the Peninsular War, and which the Spanish call the War of Independence. It has been heavily restored since.

You can make your visit more romantic by joining the nighttime visits on Wednesday or Saturday. And any day at sunset, there is no reason not to join the crowds who head to the mirador (viewpoint) at the church of San Nicolas to enjoy a panoramic view of the site.

For many visitors, the Alhambra is Granada, and having seen that, they move on. This is understandable, but they miss a lot. The end of Al-Andalus, the 800 years of Moorish rule, was the start of Spain's Golden Age, her age of empire. 1492 was of course not only the year in which Granada fell; it was also the year in which, as the rhyme says, Columbus crossed the ocean blue. The conquest and colonisation of what is now Central and South America was a disaster for the people already living there, but it generated stupendous wealth for Spain. Seville was the port through which that wealth flowed, but Granada benefited mightily as well.

Granada cathedral is a masterpiece of the Plateresque ("silversmith") style, a combination of mainstream European Renaissance proportion, intricate Muslim decoration, and Spanish austerity. Dense filigree carvings of floral and heraldic designs are marooned in great slabs of bare concrete facades.

The construction of the cathedral was authorised in that watershed year of 1492, but work did not start until 30 years later, and it took nearly two centuries to complete. The whitewashed walls and pillars, and the stained-glass windows in the cupola give the enormous building a surprising feeling of space and light. The facade was designed after the interior, and its three great arches seem too big for the square in front of them: they look over and beyond it as if they are intent on more important things than the people down below.

AVEMARIA

A couple of blocks away from the cathedral lies the Caldereria Nueva, a narrow street boasting Moroccan tea-rooms and craft shops which have been described as "the second coming of the Moors". In fact, the incomers are mostly European hippies, adherents of sufism, the mystical wing of Islam. A sufi called Sheikh Abd-Al-Qadir runs an international organisation called Mirabitun from here.

The Sheikh is actually a Scot called Ian Dallas, and rather splendidly, in a former life he is said to have co-written the screenplay of the Beatles film "Yellow Submarine".

He also gave Eric Clapton a book about a tragic romance which inspired the song "Layla".

Transcendence befitting Granada.

Seville

With 1.5 million inhabitants, Seville is Andalusia's largest city as well as its capital; indeed it is the fourth largest city in Spain. Whereas you could be forgiven for thinking that Granada and Cordoba exist mainly to service their tourist attractions, Seville is a full-on, robust and jostling city, with industrial zones, suburbs and satellite towns that don't care a hoot about your visit.

Seville is a city of intensity and contrast. The English author Laurie Lee wrote that you could "bite on the air and taste the multitudinous flavours of Spain – acid, sugary, intoxicating, sickening ... real as nowhere else."

Seville was Spain's largest and richest town in the 12th century, during the fundamentalist phase of the Moorish period, and again in the boom years of Spain's empire in the New World in the 16th and 17th centuries. It has never quite recaptured those moments of glory, but not for want of trying.

There is not much left in Seville to remind you of the Roman period, although there are impressive remains at Italica, nine kilometers away ...

... including the third-largest amphitheatre in the empire, half the size of Rome's Colosseum.

The TV series "Game of Thrones" did wonders for Andalusia's tourist industry, and Italica's amphitheatre was Dragon Pit in series 7 and 8.

The Moors left much more of an imprint, although not always in the way you expect. Seville's two main tourist sights – the Alcazar and the cathedral – are companionable neighbours, facing each other across the Plaza del Triunfo. Both of them seem more Moorish than they really are.

If you only have time to see one thing in Seville, make it the Alcazar, even if you have already visited Granada's Alhambra. The Alcazar has long been a film set, including for "Lawrence of Arabia" in 1967, and for Ridley Scott's "Kingdom of Heaven" in 2005, but its global fame was sealed by the fifth series of "Game of Thrones", so book ahead to avoid long queues. And if you go in high summer, take water: Seville is hot!

The first capital of the Moors was Cordoba, but the fundamentalist Almohads made Seville their base in the late 12th century. Little remains from the palace they built, apart from the small Patio del Yeso.

Most of the complex we can enjoy today was built for Christian rulers, but it appears Moorish because they employed Islamic craftsmen known as "mudejar", which has been variously translated as "permitted to remain", or "subjugated".

You enter the complex through the Puerta del Leon (Gate of the lion), which, unsurprisingly, has a lion above it.

You emerge into the breathtaking Patio de la Monteria. Spanish has several words for hunting, and monteria is one of them. This is one of several parts of the Alcazar which were commissioned by Peter of Castile, a controversial monarch who was dubbed both Pedro the Cruel and Pedro the Just during his 16-year reign in the mid-14th century.

The showpiece of the Alcazar's interior is the Hall of the Ambassadors, and in particular its ceiling, a mesmerising golden wooden dome containing multiple star patterns embedded with hundreds of tiny mirrors.

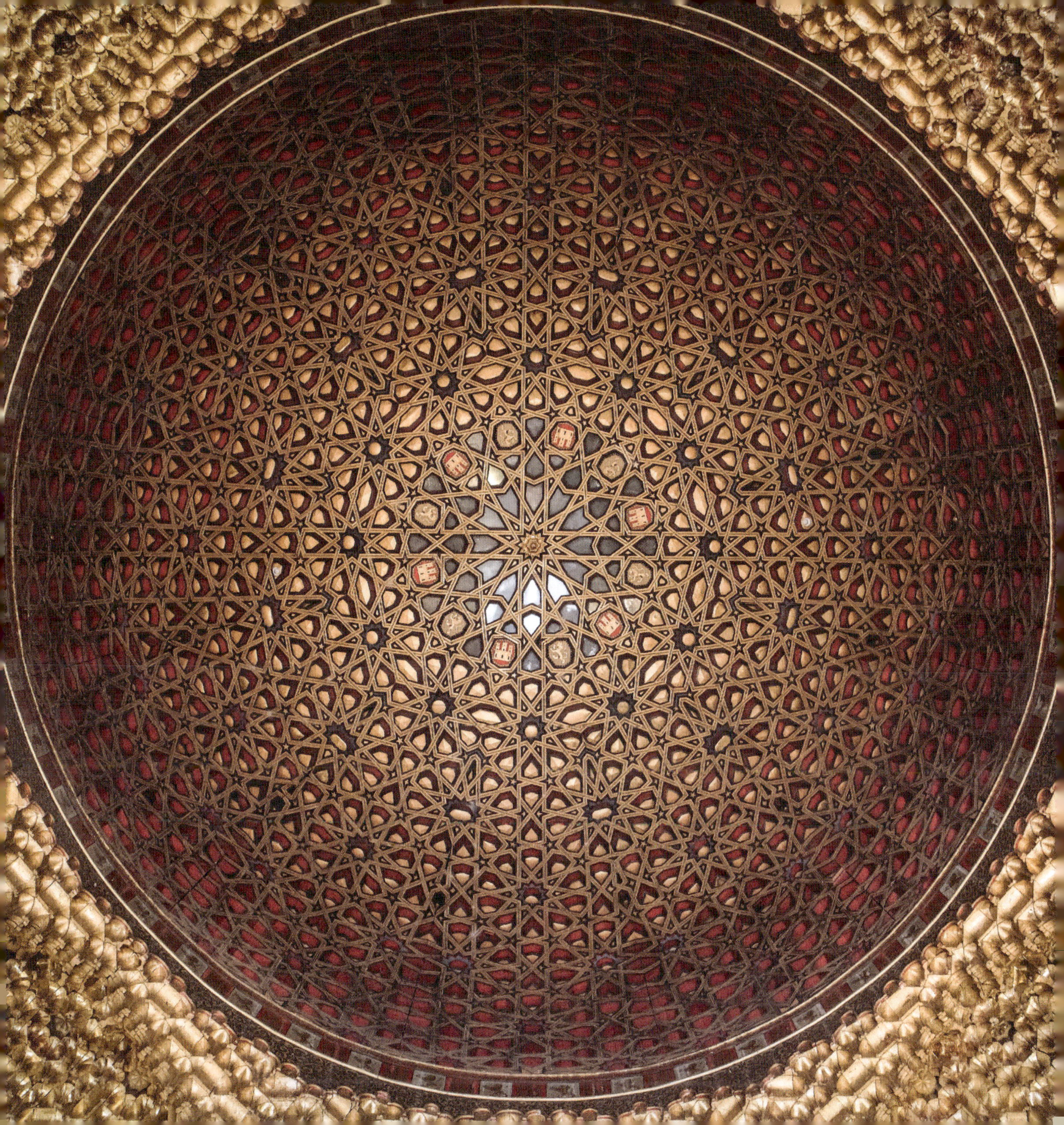

In the 16th century there were significant additions in Renaissance style, especially the gardens, where Italian designers added whimsical statues, benches, and hidden paths to the Moorish foundations of tall palm trees, pools and fountains, to produce what many regard as some of the finest gardens in Europe. After the massive earthquake of 1755, further changes were made to the buildings in the Baroque style. Fortunately, this mish-mash is a harmonious one.

Seville's cathedral has many claims to fame. It is the largest gothic cathedral in the world, and the fourth-largest church in the world overall (after St Peter's in Rome, which is 25% bigger, and churches in Brazil and Milan). But for many people its most notable feature is Moorish: the bell tower known as the Giralda.

The Giralda started life as the minaret of Seville's mosque, and it was finished exactly 50 years before the Christians captured Seville in 1248.

The surrendering Moors intended to destroy the tower to prevent it being used for blasphemous purposes, but King Alfonso X threatened to kill them all if they damaged it.

The four-story Renaissance bell-tower was added in the 16th century, and the 4m tall statue on top is a weather vane which gives the tower its name (girar is Spanish for turn). You can climb to the top of the Giralda, on a winding ramp wide enough to carry the muezzin and his guards on donkeys up to give the call to prayer. It is well worth the trouble.

Soon after Columbus' first voyage across the Atlantic, gold and silver started flowing back in huge quantities, and in 1503, Queen Isabella created the Casa de Contratacion, an organisation to oversee this trade. It designated Seville the only city permitted to receive the bounty, partly because of its superior defences, being Spain's only inland port.

Great fortunes were made by investing in voyages to extract wealth from the Americas and bring it to Spain, and also by providing goods and services to those who were doing the extracting. By 1580, Seville was the third-largest city in Europe, after Rome and Venice.

This golden age didn't last long. A plague in 1649 slashed the city's population by half, and then the river Guadalquivir silted up, and the empire trade was moved to Cadiz. During the following century, Spain started to lose her colonies, and Andalusia was especially hard hit, going from its wealthiest region to its poorest.

Tragic decline can be terribly romantic, of course, and foreign tourists, especially from Britain, began to arrive in search of not wealth, but fantasies of Arabian nights, gypsies, brigands, and sensuality. It is no coincidence that more operas are set in Seville (150!) than anywhere else in the world.

The twentieth century did Seville few favours. Franco disliked Andalusia because it had resisted his coup, and the concretisation of the Costa del Sol which he began hasn't enhanced the region's natural beauty.

The city has attempted a number of grand gestures to initiate a return to its past grandeur. It hosted two world fairs, in 1929 and 1992, which left behind some remarkable architectural play-grounds, and also substantial debts.

In 2005 the city welcomed the new century by starting construction on what is believed to be the largest wooden building in the world. The Metropol Parasol, more commonly known as Las Setas (mushrooms), was intended to revitalise a moribund part of the city. It proved as controversial as the expos, costing double the budgeted amount. It was finally completed in 2011.

Seville will probably never stop trying to recapture something of its former glories. In the meantime, the rest of us can enjoy what those glories left behind, as we meander through the narrow, winding streets of its old quarters, the wrought iron window grilles (rejas) punctuating brightly coloured walls, peeking into the fabulous private courtyards, and soaking up its heat, and its spirit of adventure and fun.

Cordoba

Of the three main cities on the Andalusian "grand tour", Cordoba probably ranks third for most people. This is not unreasonable: it is a more modest place than the other two. That being said, it was at Cordoba that Moorish Al-Andalus reached its cultural and political apogee.

Cordoba is also in some ways a more comfortable place than the other two cities. Seville is Spain's fourth-largest city, and Granada can sometimes feel over-shadowed by the huge tourist attraction that sits above it. Cordoba, by contrast, has the relaxed demeanour of a prosperous university town. The residents of its well-kept houses seem un-burdened by their town's long-ago glories, and the presence in their midst of some of Europe's finest monuments.

Cordoba's rise to fame begins with the romantic adventure story that was the life of Abd al-Rahman. In 750, he narrowly survived the massacre of his family, the Ummayads, when they were toppled as rulers of Damascus. According to one legend, Abd al-Rahman was obliged to hide under the skirts of an attractive cousin while most of his immediate family was being slaughtered around him. After several more narrow escapes, he made his way to Spain, where he gradually raised an army, and made himself emir of Al-Andalus.

Christian and Jews are considered "people of the book" by Muslims because they are mentioned in the Quran. Under Ummayad rule, they were allowed to continue practising their faiths. But if they converted, they paid less tax, which turned out to be an effective incentive for many. A famous 2002 book about Ummayad Al-Andalus, "The Ornament of the World", has the self-explanatory sub-title, How Muslims, Jews and Christians Created a Culture of Tolerance in Medieval Spain. At the turn of the first millennium, Cordoba was Europe's most populous city, with 450,000 inhabitants. It didn't last: two hundred years later that number had slumped to just 60,000.

The city's most famous monument, the great mosque, or Mezquita, was started by Abd al-Rahman, and enlarged in phases by his successors over the following two centuries. Although nowhere near the world's largest mosque, it is still considered one of the most beautiful, and among the most influential.

The forest of 850 unusual double-arched columns are made of jasper, onyx, marble and granite, the earlier ones re-used from Roman and Visigothic buildings. The lower arches are horseshoe-shaped and the upper ones are semi-circles. Their famous red stripes were inspired by the interior of Jerusalem's Dome of the Rock.

The Mezquita has a spectacular mihrab, a highly decorated decorated niche in a wall. The mihrab usually indicates the direction of Mecca, which adherents should face when praying. In Cordoba's case it doesn't, for reasons which remain uncertain.

More than five hundred years after the Mezquita was completed, it underwent an extraordinary piece of architectural surgery. Against the opposition of the city council, Charles V gave permission for the construction of a Renaissance cathedral in the heart of the mosque. Charles later regretted his decision, fearing he had authorised the destruction of something special.

The result was that for many years, Muslims and Christians worshipped in the same building, a unique outcome which seems a fitting testament to the example Cordoba once set for multiculturalism and tolerance. The building is currently only in use as a church, and moves to bring back Muslim worship there have been stymied.

A century before the collapse of the Ummayad dynasty, construction began on a new palace city, eight kilometers east of Cordoba, called Medina Azahara. It was enormous, with thousands of new houses, mosques, zoos and pleasure gardens.

It has been described as the Versailles of the Middle Ages, but it was destroyed in civil war, and was effectively lost until the 20th century, since when enough of it has been excavated and restored to make it well worth a visit.

Back in Cordoba, the Alcazar, or palace complex, is charming, if less impressive than those of Granada, Seville, or indeed Malaga. It was founded by the Ummayads, and for a time it contained the largest library in the western world. It was substantially rebuilt in the 14th century by Alfonso XI of Castile, but he used mudejar (Muslim) craftsmen, so it retains its Moorish style.

The following century, the Inquisition used it for torture and interrogation, and it is often said to be the place where Columbus finally received from Queen Isabella the backing he needed for his exploratory voyage across the Atlantic. The extensive and magnificent gardens are largely a creation of the 20th century.

No visit to Cordoba is complete without crossing the dramatic Puente Romano, especially since it is pedestrianised, and now that you can follow in the footsteps of Tyrion and Varys from "Game of Thrones".

The first stone bridge here was erected by the Romans, but most of the existing structure was built by the Ummayads. At the southern end of the bridge stands an imposing fortified gate, the Torre Calahorra.

The city of Cordoba boasts no fewer than four UN World Heritage sites, more than anywhere else in the world. (It has probably been trying a bit harder than Seville, not to mention Rome or Paris.) Joining the Medina Azahara, the Mesquita, and the old quarter where the mosque is located, the fourth is the Patios Festival.

In the first half of May, around 50 houses in the old town open the doors to their patios to the public for free. Spring is always eye-popping in Andalusia, with flowers bursting into colour like firework displays. Courtyards and secret gardens are the hidden highlight of many of its towns and cities.

Malaga

For many visitors to Andalusia, Malaga is just an airport. They land, rent a car or hop on a bus, and scoot off to one of the resorts strung out along the Costa del Sol. This is a pity: they are missing a fascinating city. It has the best-preserved of all the Moorish forts, a bewildering range of museums, including several that are world-class, and a number of architectural gems that illuminate its long and dramatic history.

The 21st century has brought major investment in Malaga's tourist industry, and it has paid returns, with many more people pausing to have a look around before heading to the beach. But perhaps because it made a late start, Malaga remains a very Spanish city, unlike its coastal neighbours to the west.

It is also Andalusia's most cosmopolitan city: while Seville is Spain's fourth-largest town, Malaga is its fourth-largest economy (after Madrid, Barcelona, and Valencia), and the largest in Andalusia.

The Phoenicians founded Malaga in the 8th century BC. They called it Malaka, either for milk, or perhaps for their god Malach. You can still see remains of Phoenician walls in the cellar of the Picasso Museum. Malaga's 2,800-year history makes it one of the oldest continuously inhabited cities in the world.

Some of that history has been bloody: Malaga has experienced some of the worst atrocities in Andalusia's often turbulent past. But it wears its scars lightly: it has an open, friendly feeling.

In the Moorish period, Malaga was often on the front line when Christian kings were expanding their influence. The Castle of Gibralfaro, and the Alcazaba fortress palace were both built during this time.

Both have been extensively restored, and the Gibralfaro in particular is a picturesque delight to wander around, and refreshingly un-crowded. The views of the port and the city down below are superb. The Roman theatre which lies at the feet of the Moorish buildings is less well preserved.

When Queen Isabella and King Ferdinand, the Catholic Kings, were campaigning to clear the Moors out of Granada province, their last foothold in Spain, the battle for Malaga was gruesome. It was the world's first conflict where gunpowder was used by both sides, and the defenders eventually gave up when a three-month siege brought them to the point of starvation. The punishment for their valiant defence was that all but 50 of them were enslaved. The rest of Granada took note, and negotiated quicker and less painful surrenders.

A generation after this invasion, work began on Malaga's cathedral. The initial designs were in the Renaissance style, but lack of funds delayed construction, and by the time it got going again, tastes had changed, so the facade is Baroque instead. Only one of the two intended towers was built, so the cathedral is known as "La Manquita", the one-armed woman.

One reason why the funds ran out is that money was diverted to help the US colonies break away from Britain in the American Revolution.

The British seizure of Gibraltar in 1704 meant Malaga became Spain's main fortified port on the Mediterranean.

Then came industrialisation, and Malaga still boasts many tall brick chimneys from the days when it was second only to Barcelona as a manufacturing centre. New railways arrived, bringing new financial institutions, and new arts buildings.

By the late 19th century, however, Malaga was failing to compete with the economic powerhouses in northern Spain, and in 1937, during the Civil War, the city suffered another brutal invasion. Franco's fascist allies from Italy and Germany pounded the city they derided as "Red Malaga", and of the 50,000 people who fled towards Almeria, more than 7,000 were slaughtered.

The most recent invasion of Malaga has been far less unkind. The influx of tourists was ignited by the opening in 2003 of the Museo Picasso Málaga, just 200 metres from where the artist was born. 285 of his works hang in the converted Buenavista Palace, which dates back to the first half of the 16th century.

Among the other 30-odd museums which have sprouted in Malaga, our favourite is the Automotive Museum, which is home to 100 vintage cars, one of the most important collections in the world. We are not petrol heads, but the Portuguese enthusiast Joao Magalhaes assembled works of supreme craftsmanship from the factories of Hispano Suiza, Bugatti, Rolls Royce, Bentley, Jaguar, Ferrari, and of course Aston Martin. And what makes this museum really special is the clever way the cars are placed in context: most are accompanied by stylish mannequins dressed in the costumes of their era.

When you have exhausted yourself with touring Moorish castles, Renaissance cathedrals, and museums, you can relax by strolling through the Paseo del Parque, a beautiful promenade park with palm trees and statues...

... and then refuel with the local delicacy of espetos, sardines grilled over open fires in the chiringuitos on Malaga's famous beaches.

Ronda

There is underground parking in the centre of Ronda, but that is cheating. If you can, find a parking space outside the city walls, and enter Ronda through the Puerta (gate) de Almocabar. Walk up the hill towards the centre, and take a left off Calle Espiritu Santu into the wonderful Plaza de la Duquesa de Parcent.

Parcent is an extremely modest town in the province of Alicante, so it is curious that one of the most beautiful squares in all of Spain is named after it.

In fact, the plaza takes its title from the second duchess of Parcent, the splendidly named Trinidad Von Scholtz-Hermensdorff, who was born in Malaga, and went on to become one of the first women members of the Spanish Congress, in 1927.

One of the architectural stars of the square is the Iglesia de Santa Maria del Mayor, whose exquisite belltower has been described as a Renaissance version of Disneyland. This church took more than 200 years to build, and is Ronda's main places of worship, although it is not a cathedral.

Along a neighbouring side of the square lies a handsome colonaded building which today houses the ayuntamiento, or town council, but was originally a prison.

The centre of the plaza boasts a collection of fine trees providing welcome shade in the summer.

You can continue towards the town centre by heading back to the main street, the Calle Arminan, but better, you can wind your way parallel to it through the back streets which contain many fine old houses. After a few beguiling minutes you will spill out onto the Puente Nuevo.

This is Ronda's spectacular set-piece, and it is a full-on Lord of the Rings experience. The "new bridge" was completed in 1793, and spans a 120-metre drop. A single-arch bridge which preceded it collapsed in 1741, killing 50 people. The current structure is breathtaking, but it has witnessed some grisly episodes. During the Civil War, the room above the central arch was used as a torture chamber by both sides, who flung their victims down into the gorge after extracting whatever information (or revenge) they were after.

As you walk across the bridge you can give yourself some world-class vertigo by peering over the edges into the film set scenes below. You can also walk underneath the bridge along the Guadalevin river, and this is definitely worth doing.

Beyond the Puenta Nueva lies the Plaza de España, flanked by impressive buildings, and surrounded by a rash of restaurants and tourist shops to satisfy the appetites of the hordes of tourists who descend on Ronda in the summer months.

The grandest building is the Parador de Ronda, one of Spain's chain of luxury hotels that occupy historic buildings – in this case a former town hall. As well as luxury, this one boasts stupendous views across and down into the gorge.

As it crosses the Plaza de España, Calle Arminan transubstantiates into the Calle Virgen de la Paz, and this takes you on to the the Plaza de Toros de Ronda – Ronda's famous bullring, which is well worth the modest price of admission.

Ronda has a claim to be the birthplace of modern bullfighting. For centuries, bulls were fought on horseback, but in the mid-nineteenth century, lone matadors on foot began to face the animal with just a short sword and a cape.

A display inside the bullring contrasts the authenticity, severity and aplomb of the Ronda school with the ostentatious displays, swerves and bold stances characteristic of the Seville tradition. Presumably the bull, weakened by the picadors' lances, completely fails to appreciate these finer stylistic flourishes.

The stadium is reminiscent of the Colosseum in Rome, but the preparation areas are all above ground, not in catacombs as in Rome. The stockyards and alleys where the bulls are enraged and channelled are scrupulously clean, but it is not hard to imagine the pain and the horror they have witnessed.

Two families, the Romeros and the Ordonez, have provided Ronda's most famous bullfighters. Pedro Romero (1754-1839) killed 5,558 bulls without suffering serious injury himself.

Away from the bullring, the Plaza de Toros contains the Escuela de Equitacion RMR, the oldest riding school in Spain, and the second-oldest in Europe (after the Spanish school in Vienna). It also houses displays of riding gear, vintage rifles and pistols, and a fascinating exhibition of duelling equipment and accessories. As is often the case in Spain, the notices by the displays are concise and informative, and the English translations are close to perfect.

There is a great deal more still to see in Ronda, notably the 14th-century Arab baths by the lower entrance to the city, and the Mondragon Palace, with its Moorish courtyards, its stunning views and a genuinely fascinating museum.

And just 20km north-west of Ronda lies Acinipo, which was once a major Roman town, and is now the superb location of a well-preserved Roman theatre.

Cadiz

For many people, San Sebastian, up north in Basque country, is the apogee of Spanish food culture. Back when daytime drinking was still a thing, and one round lettuce leaf with some cucumber slices and a tomato were considered to be a salad, the BBC filmed Keith Floyd swerving among the pintxos bars, daring us to sample the strange and exotic nibbles made from alien ingredients – such as anchovies and olives. Two decades later, the Beeb served up San Sebastian again, to an audience that had become far more sophisticated. The food was less shocking, and the chef – Rick Stein this time – was a much safer pair of hands. But San Sebastian remained the star of the show.

Cadiz is Andalusia's answer to San Sebastian. It has the same picturesque and labyrinthine lanes, it is similarly dotted with bars and restaurants, and it boasts a similarly dramatic bay, dominated by a show-stopper of a cathedral that would not look out of place in Renaissance Italy.

The Cadiz menu is dominated by fresh fish, and possibly the best time of year to visit is during tuna season. Along the Costa de la Luz, tuna is still caught in the time-honoured manner established by the Phoenicians – the fish are trapped between April and June, as they migrate from the Atlantic to the Mediterranean on their way to spawn. Fresh Cadiz tuna is unlike any tuna you have eaten elsewhere – unctuous, and melt-in-the-mouth delicious – so far from British supermarkets' cardboard offerings as to be unrecognisable.

Andalusian pescaito frito is ubiquitous, and available all year round. Fish fresh from the sea, dusted lightly in flour and flash-fried – a simple treat to challenge any Michelin-starred offering, and available every few tens of metres in any direction. Being just a few miles from Jerez and Sanlucar, sherry is a common accompaniment to any meal in Cadiz. Local Manzanilla is recommended as the perfect partner to local Sanlucar prawns – the only prawn in Spain with a designation of origin.

Cadiz is probably the oldest continuously inhabited city in Western Europe. It was founded by the Phoenicians in 1104 BC, and was important to both the Carthaginians and then the Romans. A Roman theatre re-discovered as recently as 1980 was one of the largest in the ancient world. During the reign of the emperor Augustus, Cadiz was home to more wealthy Roman citizens than any city other than Padua in northern Italy, and Rome itself.

Entertainment was important to this community, and the dancing girls of Cadiz acquired a reputation for licentious performances. It is perhaps no coincidence that Cadiz's Fiesta each February is a highlight of the Andalusian calendar, although levity and liveliness has replaced the lewdness.

GRAN TEATRO FALLA
FESTIVAL IBEROAMERICANO DE TEATRO
de·cadiz
FESTIVAL IBEROAMERICANO DE TEATRO
de·cadiz

Cadiz played little part in the 800-year history of Al-Andalus, so it boasts no important Moorish or mudejar architecture. It became significant again in the Age of Exploration which followed the expulsion of the Moors, especially after 1717, when Seville's Guadalquivir river silted up, and the government made Cadiz the port of disembarkation for all the gold and silver flowing into Spain from the Americas.

This made Cadiz a target for English naval attacks, and later on it was beseiged by the French during the Napoleonic Wars.

In 1812, Cadiz made another appearance on the national stage, when it briefly hosted the Spanish parliament, or Cortes, in the Plaza San Antonio. A constitutional document was proclaimed there which contained the world's first use of the word "liberal" in a political context.

A rather grandiose Monument to the Constitution of 1812 was built a century later in the Plaza de Espana.

Today, Cadiz is characterised by faded elegance, and it is experiencing demographic decline. The Oriel windows are still there, and the tiled courtyards still peep our from behind heavy double wooden doors. But many of the 160 towers which merchants built on their townhouses to look out for their ships have disappeared.

The palm-fringed plazas, and the charming townhouses that pack together and create the maze of narrow streets of the old town attract fewer tourists than the Moorish set pieces in the larger cities of the Andalusian Grand Tour. Those who do come here are usually enchanted. Being located on a narrow peninsula attached to the mainland by a thin strip of land means that nowhere in Cadiz is far from the sea – and we do all love to be beside the seaside.

Villages and countryside

Pueblos Blancos

The famous "white villages" of Andalusia mostly cluster in Cadiz province and in the southern part of Malaga province. To qualify as a pueblo blanco, a village should comprise modest, whitewashed boxy houses with terracotta tiled roofs, and be presided over by a church and a castle. The village should also be cacophonous, with a soundtrack of dogs, cockerels, donkeys, shouting and laughter, children playing, a soupcon of Spanish gangsta rap, occasional gunfire (or fire crackers), and the odd rev of a quad bike.

To be fair, these secondary auditory characteristics are less true of the premier league villages – the names found in the list of "pueblos mas bonitos de España" – where we begrudgingly concede that the pop of cava corks and classical flamenco guitar is a more common leitmotif.

Over time, tour operators have seen fit to string together the main clusters of pueblos blancos, packaging them into branded routes and, as in the Luberon, Chianti, and the Cotswolds, a self-drive week "collecting" pueblos blancos is a delightful and well-established Andalusian immersion holiday.

Originally, pueblos blancos were often settled by the families and descendants of the Berber warriors who came to Andalusia in the 8th century.

As mentioned, most villages contain forts or castles, sometimes based on long-abandoned Roman forts. Their locations were chosen because they were easily defended: they were often on the front line between Al-Andalus and the Christian kingdoms – hence the "de la Frontera" in some of their names. So they usually enjoy dramatic views of the surrounding countryside, being slung like hammocks between peaks, or strung around mountainsides like pearl necklaces.

Their mountainous locations also dictate the architecture, which features steep, winding alleyways of cobbled streets – although the cobbles are increasingly being replaced by more shoe-friendly surfaces. Windows are protected by graceful wrought iron (originally, according to romantic legend, to protect the virtue of the young ladies of the house) and archways support many of the walls.

Most of the pueblos blancos have a small town square of some sort, and a church dating to the 16th century.

Village life is played out in the little shops, the tapas bars and, in the larger towns, the restaurants, which are fabulous places to eat and drink under the azure blue sky.

Their name comes from the ubiquitous whitewash, which is renewed on each house every few years after the spring rains have finished. The white comes from the lime used in the whitewash: in the campo around the villages you can find kilns where the lime was heated and prepared. The white makes a superb background for the bright colours of the flowers which the houseproud villagers display.

Many of the pueblos blancos were abandoned in the 16th century, when the Christians evicted the moriscos, and it took a while before Christian families moved in. In recent years their populations have dwindled again, as young people leave to find work in the towns and cities on the coast. The regional government is making serious attempts to arrest and reverse this decline, investing in the villages' rich tourist potential.

The closer to the Costa del Sol, the more touristic the village: if you like peace and quiet, then visit villages a good way back from the coastal front line.

Andalusia's pueblo blancos are marvellous bases for hiking, horseriding, and cycling, and for the more adventurous among you, there is also climbing, potholing, and paragliding. Oh, and the sunsets can be pretty impressive, too.

Zahara de la Sierra

Flying south over Andalusia into Malaga provides a birds-eye view of two contrasting but intriguing landscapes. First, the olive groves of Jaen province, a patchwork pixelated cartoon like a Roy Lichtenstein painting. Look away for five minutes and they are still there: Spain grows the olives for 40% of the world's olive oil production, and Jaen is where she keeps her olive trees!

Second, the turquoise reservoirs of inland Andalusia – little fragments of a Bora Bora blue lagoon. The view of tropical beaches from 30,000 feet is quite a lure, and happily, Zahara de la Sierra features on most pueblo blanco 'top ten' lists as well as presiding over the Zahara-El Gastor reservoir.

Driving to Zahara from Ronda, the nearest town, you could take the A-2300, hugging the shores of the hidden reservoir, and arriving below the village with only a short, safe drive up to its lower levels.

Ho hum.

Alternatively, pour yourself a strong coffee and knock back a travel sickness pill, breathe in, and execute a (mostly) controlled hairpin descent on the CA-9104 from the mountains that lie between Zahara and its near neighbour Grazalema. Wow! Now THAT is the way to arrive. It takes an extra 30 minutes, but it is just so worth it.

The narrow road doesn't afford any opportunities to stop and take in the incredible views, so you may well feel a toddler's urge to shout "Again! again!" when you get to the bottom.

Both Robert Louis Stephenson and the lord Buddha are credited with saying that the journey is every bit as important as the destination; perhaps they had just visited Zahara. The tantalising, spectacular views of the brilliant lake below will make you gasp, even as the frankly bonkers profile of the road on Google Maps makes you laugh out loud.

Walking around the smart village of Zahara itself, you find the classic ingredients of premier league pueblo blanco: immaculate whitewash, artisanal terracotta, neat stone mosaic paving, and accents of black metal work in windows and as signage. Zahara boasts a run of stylish pavement cafes, some good churches, and a well-restored castle.

Beware the manageable but slippery hike up to the castle from the village: on a ski slope it would be a red run. The climb is well worth it for the great views of the landscape and lake below, framed beautifully by the castle's glassless stone windows.

The dam that created the reservoir is one of several interruptions to the 172km journey of the Guadalete river as it meanders down from the Sierra de Grazalema, ultimately emptying into the Atlantic in the Bay of Cadiz. The Guadalete dam was completed in the winter of 1991, and is one of around 1,200 similar dam projects in Spain.

Many of the rivers in this region have romantic Moorish names. Guadalete is an Arabic/Greek cut-and-shut: "wadj al-Lethe", or "wadi Lethe", means "River of Forgetfulness". A little further south, running from Ronda to the Mediterranean, is the Guadiaro, or the "River of Gold".

JÚZCAR,
EL PRIMER PUEBLO PITUFO
DEL MUNDO.
16 DE JUNIO DE 2011
SONY PICTURES
animation
SMURF, and all Smurfs characters:
©Peyo. All Rights Reserved. "Smurf" and "The Smurfs"
are registered trademarks of STUDIO PEYO.
COLUMBIA
PICTURES
www.LosPitufos3D.com

Juzcar – the Smurf village

The thing about the "white villages" of the Andalusian mountains is that they are white. All their walls are painted white, or "whitewashed", with slaked lime (calcium hydroxide, or CaOH2, since you ask) and chalk, and their roofs are terracotta tiles.

All except one. There is a corner of Andalusia which is forever blue.

It's called Júzcar, and it proudly proclaims itself the world's first Smurf village. It's probably the last, too, for reasons that will become clear.

It's all thanks to Sony Pictures, who released a blockbuster movie in 2011 called "The Smurfs in 3D", capitalising on the enormous entertainment value of a race of small blue creatures (three apples high) with three fingers on each hand, and annoying squeaky voices.

Brits like to blame the Belgians for the existence of Smurfs, but Peyo was just the pen-name of their creator. His real name was Pierre Culliford, and that surname betrays an English father. So if you are British, wipe that smirk off your face.

Peyo invented the creatures while dining with a friend. He temporarily forgot the name for salt, and asked his friend to pass the schtroumpf. They both thought this was very funny (you probably had to be there), and Peyo began to weave a story world around it. Schtroumpf became Smurf in Dutch, and also in English, but in Spain they were re-named Pitufo.

Smurfs went on to become ridiculously lucrative, appearing in comics, TV shows, video games, theme parks, ice dancing shows, genuine Belgian coins, and, of course, merchandising. Lots and lots of merchandising.

Some people take Smurfs more seriously than they really should. They are called sociologists. There is a lively debate, apparently, about whether the 100-plus Smurf characters inhabit a socialist paradise, or a racist and totalitarian dictatorship.

The most recent contribution to this strand of academic debate (presumably funded by taxpayers somewhere) is a scholarly warning about the intellectual danger of basing cultural critiques on cartoon creatures.

The rights to make a Smurf film were acquired by producer Jordan Kemer in 2002 after five years of negotiations. He spent another six years developing the movie with Paramount Pictures and then Nickelodeon Movies, before finally clinching a deal with Sony Pictures in 2008. Filming started in New York in 2010.

In spring 2011, Sony approached Júzcar's mayor with what must have seemed a very bizarre request: to paint their sleepy white village blue in order to promote the movie. The 240 residents of the village held a meeting and voted to accept, with just one dissenting voice.

That must have been an intriguing meeting, but the really interesting conversation to eavesdrop would have been the one where the film-makers sought – and obtained – permission from the Bishop of Malaga to paint their church Smurf blue. All in all, it took 4,000 litres of paint to transform Júzcar into "el primer pueblo Pitufo del mundo".

The villagers only agreed to Sony's request on condition that Sony would pay for the houses to be painted white again afterwards, but when they received 80,000 visitors in the six months after the movie opened, they took another vote, and decided to stay blue. Many of the residents found they could start businesses as tour guides, and vendors of Smurf merchandise.

The critics were unimpressed when the movie came out, with one remarking that the director could have made it in "in his sleep, which is where all but the most attentive of caregivers will find themselves drifting." But who cares what the critics think: the movie was a big commercial success, grossing a total of $564 million on a budget of $110 million. On its opening weekend it vied for box office supremacy with the almost equally bizarre, genre-blending movie "Cowboys and Aliens".

With commercial success like that, a sequel was inevitable, and Júzcar's blue walls were given a fresh coat in 2013 in order to welcome "The Smurfs 2: Nice Gets Naughty" into the world. The critics were even less impressed than before, complaining that it had "everything you hated about the first movie, and more." One opined that "The Smurfs 2 will keep a child reasonably entertained for 105 minutes—but so will a large, empty cardboard box. The box is more likely to stimulate the child's imagination, and less likely to contain jokes about testicles."

The accountants were also unimpressed this time, as box office takings were $200 million down on the first instalment, so there were several false starts before the third movie, "The Smurfs: The Lost Village", appeared in 2017.

The critics remained ... well, critical, with one cynic describing it as "a mediocre effort that nonetheless succeeds in its main goal of keeping its blue characters alive for future merchandising purposes."

Which should have been great news for the good people of Júzcar, but unfortunately by this time they had fallen out with the heirs to Peyo's estate, who wanted Júzcar to pay them 12% of all profits made from goods and services using their intellectual property. The villagers refused, and so in August 2017 they lost the right to call Júzcar the Smurf village.

At the time of writing there are still a few murals on less prominent walls, and a few giant plastic Smurfs tucked away in discreet corners in case an inspector from the World Intellectual Property Office comes snooping. There are several curated and numbered 'senderos' (routes) to follow, including one that takes in the various murals – some of which are more expertly executed than others.

The village is hilly, and a tour on foot is a 30-minute stroll with farly steep ups and downs. Were it not for the tight security, you could avail yourself of a genuinely impressive zipwire (Disney meets Mad Max) and have the whole *Júzcar* experience in a matter of seconds. Bring your own harness and carabiners!

And if the worst should come to the worst on the zipwire, your relatives will take comfort from the fact that the village cemetery is the only building that was never painted blue.

Júzcar is – mercifully, some might say – hidden away from most vantage points in the Genal valley. Driving from Alpandeire to Júzcar funnels you down a ricocheting, narrowing track, at first too narrow for two vehicles and ultimately, it feels, too narrow for one vehicle.

If you have a strong constitution, the journey is a treat, but if you have a weak stomach, a trip to see the Smurfs is not for you... and the drive is pretty challenging, too.

Hiking in Andalusia

A guest article by our friend Patrick Elvin, who has lived in the Serrenia de Ronda for almost 25 years, and has published eight books on hiking in Andalusia. It is an understatement to say that Patrick is an enthusiastic walker: he has been a guide and an inspiration to thousands of other walkers.

Description

Andalusia boasts some of the most dramatic and varied landscapes in the world, with mountains and meadows, wildlife and waterfalls, forests and fell. The views change all the time: they are never less than enchanting, and they are frequently breathtaking.

But beware: footpaths can often be stony and overgrown, so good walking boots are recommended. It is hot in the summer, so wear a hat, and carry lots of water.

Flora and fauna

Much of the landscape is uncultivated, used only for grazing, predominately by sheep goats pigs and cattle. The wild flowers are varied and spectacular, especially in the spring. Most of the trees are evergreen, so the general impression is of green all year round. The pines can seem electric against the hot blue sky.

Much of Andalusia is used for growing olives, and the provinces of Cordoba, Granada, and Jaen in particular have expansive olive tree plantations at lower levels. In the cork-growing south, when the cork is stripped from the trees, it leaves them a vibrant red.

Deer, ibex and wild pigs are the main wildlife, and herds of goats and sheep roam freely. You will often see large raptors such as eagles and vultures. The endangered lynx is making a comeback in a reserve near Cordoba.

Weather and seasons

The weather ranges from snow in the higher mountains in the winter, to very high temperatures in the summer. The best season for walking is the spring months of April, May, and June, when the temperatures are steady between 20 and 30. It rarely rains, and the countryside is at its technicolour best. In July and August, most people restrict their walking to the early morning.

September brings blessed relief from the heat, and October and November usually bring some much-needed rain, with great walking conditions in between. Even in midwinter you are warm in the sunshine, and the sun shines on 320 days each year. Note that especially in the mountainous areas, it can rain at short notice, and weather forecasts can be inaccurate.

Pathfinding

The authorities in Andalusia have been relatively slow to recognise the value of hiking for health and also for tourism, but they are now gradually signposting both long distance routes and local walks. The markings vary from sturdy, professional-looking signposts, to painted stripes on rocks and trees. The three main types of path are:

GR (Gran Recorrido) long distance paths, marked red and white.

PR (Pequeño Recorrido) shorter paths connecting villages, marked yellow and white.

SL (Sendero Local) local paths, marked green and white.

Wikiloc is an excellent resource for hikers which has become increasingly popular in recent years. It is a website and an app, developed in Barcelona, and available in Spanish and English versions. It contains an estimated 500,000 walks in Andalusia alone. If you follow a route which someone else has uploaded, the app will alert you when you diverge from the path. This is invaluable in the more overgrown areas, and means you never need to worry again about getting seriously lost. You can also record your own routes for future reference, and to share with friends.

Another useful resource which is gaining awareness is What3Words, an app whose developers have given a three-word address to every square meter on the earth's surface. Armed with one of these addresses and a GPS device, you can find any location. GPS does not require internet or mobile phone connection. If you get separated from your hiking companions and they can send you their current address, you can save yourselves a lot of time and frustration.

Don't forget to leave gates as you found them. They vary widely, from modern, electrically-operated affairs, to old bedsteads, and confections of wire and rope.

The areas

The main walking areas are spread across 24 National and Natural Parks. These Parks reflect the varied geography of the area: a low-lying mountain range in the north (the Sierra Morena), higher mountain ranges in the centre which feed the mighty Guadalquiver basin where Sevilla and Cordoba are located, and to the east, Spain's most impressive mountain range, containing the highest mainland mountain, Mulhacen. In addition there are two coastal parks. Most parks have leaflets and booklets on the main walks in their areas.

Here are the nine principal areas:

Sierra Nevada: steep-sided valleys, and seven peaks of over 3,000 metres.

Cazorla: the source of the Guadalquivir, with wooded slopes leading to ranges of over 2,000 metres. There is an iconic walk up the Rio Barrosa.

Alcornocales: rolling hills containing huge swathes of corkwoods, and scattered vllages with low population density. At 174,000 hectares, this is the largest cork forested park in the Iberian Peninsular. Noted for its cave paintings. At the north end, the Sierra de Grazalema records the highest annual rainfall in Spain, and the famous Pinsapo pine is found here.

Cota Doñana: a world-renowned nature reserve.

Magina and Subbeticca: massive mountains rising out of the plains of the Guadalquivir to the north.

Aracena: lower hills studded with attractive villages, linked by paths flanked by ancient stone walls.

Cabo de Gata: a spectacular coastline with sandy bays and steep-sided cliffs.

Sierra de las Nieves: contains the impressive mass of Torrecilla and other peaks.

Almijara: steep-sided mountains including la Maroma, the highest mountain in Malaga province, and some very pretty villages.

Long distance footpaths

These make ideal settings for day walks, or walking holidays covering longer stretches of the route. The most important and interesting are:

GR7: runs from Tarifa to Andorra, and crosses Andalusia from south-west to north-east. It splits into two parallel routes near Antequera. The best parts lie south of Ronda, in the Alpujarras, Cazorla, and Sierra Magina.

GR 48: runs for 571 kilometers from Portugal along the northern part of Andalusia through the Sierra Morena and Cordoba, and finishes at the town of Santa Elena.

GR 240: a spectacular long-distance path which runs 300 kilometers around the Sierra Nevada at an average height of 2,000 metres. This is only for experienced walkers, as it passes through no villages on the entire route.

GR 249: a 35-stage, 670 kilometer circumnavigation of Malaga Province. The best parts are stages 1 – 10 between Nerja and Alfarnatejo, and stages 24 – 28 south of Ronda.

GR 141: a circular path from Ronda to Gaucin via the Guadiaro valley, returning via the Genal valley. It takes in nine of the Serrania de Ronda pueblos blancos. Six stages and 116 kilometers.

GR 140: runs from Cabo de Gata to Puerto de la Ragua. Ten stages and 160 kilometers over the Sierra Alhamilla, then through spaghetti western country, and finally between Sierra Gador and the Sierra Nevada, rising to 2,000 metres.

The Via de la Plata: a pilgrimage route from Sevilla to Santiago. It traverses the Sierra Morena leaving Andalusia just south of Monesterio. Stages 2 and 3 are the most highly recommended. The Camino Mozarabe is an offshoot of the Via de la Plata, running from various provincial capitals, (Almeria, Malaga, Jaen, and Granada) and converging near Cordoba to continue to Merida, where it joins up with the Via de la Plata. The Almeria – Granada section passes through the interesting towns of Moclin, Alcala la Real, Baena and Castro del Rio.

Riding in Andalusia

A guest article by our friend Clare Copeman, a true Renaissance woman who divides her time between Gaucin and London. She is a superb horsewoman, and knows far more about equestrian sports than we ever will.

The Andalusian horse is known as the 'pura raza española' (pure Spanish horse), a breed which has lived in the Iberian Peninsula for thousands of years. It is typically a strong animal, docile but intelligent, with a long, thick mane and tail. In the centuries before warfare was mechanised, it was much prized as a war horse.

Ask any Andalusian about his horse and he will proudly tell you is how noble it is. Horses feature prominently in every Andalucian festival, event and parade. They accompany the statues of village saints on their annual 'Romeria', when they are taken into the countryside for a day of feasting and celebration. The horse is the star of many 'Ferias', strutting his stuff alongside his proud owner. In re-enactments of Napoleonic invasions, and famous rides such as the yearly 'Ruta Romantica', horses play an important role. And of course it is almost always horses who carry the Three Kings through town streets on the eve of January 6th to spread Christmas cheer and distribute presents to the children.

Jerez is the epicentre of Andalusia's equestrian art. The Royal School there gives weekly exhibitions in a palace in the centre of the city. To book this wonderful spectacle, called 'See How Our Horses Dance', go to their website:

http://entradas.realescuela.org/en/

Another Jerez highlight is the horse festival in May, when more than a thousand horses are brought together.

It is a magical spectacle, with everyone in traditional Spanish costume: ladies riding side-saddle in brightly coloured flamenco dresses, and men in high-waisted trousers, waistcoats, and short jackets.

The riders wear sombreros, and the drivers of the many beautiful carriages wear Calanes hats, which are round, and made of velvet or moulded felt, with an upturned brim, and worn over a cotton handkerchief tied with a pirate knot at the back.

The festival takes place in the González Hontoria Park, and features superb displays of horsemanship, 'vaquero' (cowboy) and classical dressage, riding competitions, polo, fabulous carriage driving, flamenco, and bull fights.

Riding in Andalusia is one of the great pleasures in life. As you will have seen and read in this book, the scenery here is stunning, and what better way to view it than riding one of the local Andalusian or Hispanic Arab horses. As well as being intelligent, these horses are very sure footed, which is essential to cope with some of the mountainous terrain.

AGETREA, the Andalusian Rural and Equestrian Tourism Entrepreneurs Association, has more than 20 member centres. Its website is https://www.andaluciacaballo.org/

Here is a list of some of the ones that I have personally enjoyed and recommend, going from West to East.

Los Barrios, Cadiz. Jesus Sevilla organises rides along the Atlantic coast. A very pleasurable three-day ride is from Tarifa along the beaches to Zahara de los Atunas. The ride takes you through the umbrella pines, and there are picnic lunches and BBQs cooked on the beach.

The horses love the soft sand underfoot after the rocky terrain they are more used to. You can really let your horse go, and gallop for miles along the beach. January is a good month to do this as the beaches are not crowded. Jesus is also a walking and cycling guide. Email: jesussevilla08@hotmail.com

Osuna, Seville. Jesus Sanchez arranges rides for a few hours, or four-night journeys along the Royal Way to Ronda, starting in the beautiful city of Osuna north of Ronda. The Osuna bull ring was used in the film 'A Game of Thrones', and is well worth a visit before you set off.

You ride through typical Sevillian countryside: olive groves, wheat fields and scrubland.

As you head south towards your destination you pass cattle ranches, a 19th century Hermitage, a 16th century Convent, and a wine cellar where you can taste the wines. At last, you enter the gorge of Ronda, and ride up to the bull ring. The overnight accommodation is in charming rural hotels, and the days are broken up with mid-morning snacks and picnic lunches to give both you and the horse some rest.

http://www.turisnoruralosuna. com/de-osuna-a-ronda-a-caballo

Gaucín, Malaga. There is no longer an official riding company in Gaucín, but both Clare Arbuthnot on +34 658 227 735 and Karen Considine on +34 633 155 537 occasionally take people riding. For this you need your own insurance.

With the dramatic Serrania de Ronda as a backdrop, you ride through the cork forests along wide tracks. In the spring you will inhale wonderful scents of wild lavender and sweet chestnut, and in June you might see the cork cutters loading up their mules with cork.

An evening ride down to the Genal river across the large estates of Almuña and La Hoya is beautiful. As the summer progresses, both horses and riders will prefer rides in the early morning or in the evening.

Casares, Malaga. Fun in the Sun organises rides by the hour, and is particularly good for beginners. http://www.ridingfuninthesun.com

Hinojares, Jaen. Jose Coronada arranges rides which range from a couple of hours to a week. He is based in the wonderful Sierra de Cazorla Natural Park (2,099 sq.kms.), a UNESCO site. He uses English saddles, and as with any riding holiday, you must be able to walk, trot and canter.

One of his excursions starts from the village of Hinojares. You ride through olive groves and down to lush rivers, waterfalls and backwaters. You climb from 900m to 1,800m to the heart of the Sierra de Cazorla. This is where the expertise of the horses really shows. From the moment they are born, they learn to pick their hooves up high so that they don't stumble on the steep, rocky, narrow paths. You will explore creeks and gorges. After a slight descent you come to the Guadalentin River, a historic place where Moors and Christians fought one of the most important battles during the campaign to conquer the Kingdom of Granada.

A night is spent in the comfortable Parador Nacional, formerly one of Franco's hunting lodges. Climbing from the Rio Guadalquivir, you get wonderful views of the village of Cazorla. Descending to the river again, you ride into the foothills of the mountain range of the Agrios to reach the Port of Tiscar, where two navigation towers mark the mid 13th century border between the Nazrid Kingdom of Granada and the kingdoms of Murcia, Jaen, Cordoba and Seville. You picnic at the source of the River Guadalquivir, before returning through charming villages to return to Hinojares. http://www.cazorlavatur.com. Instagram: rutasacaballocazorla.

Finally, polo is a popular sport in Andalusia, and the Santa Maria Polo Club in Sotogrande (Costa del Sol) stages matches in late July and August. Self-proclaimed as the Wimbledon of polo, it is one of the best clubs in continental Europe, with four world-class grounds and teams.

Caminito del Rey

We first saw the Caminito del Rey (the King's little path) from a train, going from Malaga to Seville. We didn't know what we were looking at, but we were astonished, and immediately decided that one day we would explore this improbable, ambitious, and audacious trail. When we did, we discovered that the reverse view – of a train from the walkway – is equally spectacular. The railway hugs the sheer mountainside, and trains dive into and out of tunnels like needles doing embroidery.

Work started on the original walkway, known without the diminutive ending as the Camino del Rey, in 1901, and it was opened four years later. It was not built for tourists, but for engineers who needed to travel between the Chorro and Gaitanejo waterfalls, which fed the El Chorro Power Plant.

For several stretches, the walkway is suspended 105 metres up a sheer rock face. There are stories that it was built by prisoners on death row, but in fact, the construction force was mostly sailors from Malaga, who were accustomed to working while suspended from ropes.

In 1921, with great fanfare, Alfonso XIII visited the walkway, and it acquired its current name.

This Alfonso has a curious biography. His father died while his mother was still pregnant, so he became king the day he was born. He fell in love with a granddaughter of Queen Victoria, who converted to Catholicism to marry him, in the face of opposition from both their families.

He later distanced himself from her because she carried a haemophiliac gene, which their sons inherited. He supported the dictator Manuel Primo de Rivera, and became so unpopular that he had to leave the country in 1931 to avoid a civil war, leaving Spain without a king until 1975. Nevertheless, he is the only monarch ever to be nominated for the Nobel Peace Prize. (That was in 1917, and he came second to The Red Cross.)

The walkway hosted celebrities of a different kind in 1959, when it was one of the locations for a major Hollywood movie, "The Scent of Mystery", starring Elizabeth Taylor, Peter Lorre, and Denholm Elliot.

The film was a commercial and critical flop, and would be entirely forgotten by now, if it had not been the only movie ever to use the Smell-O-Vision system, in which theatres were sprayed with changing perfumes in synch with the plot – like coffee, petrol, gunpowder, tobacco (for the villain) and perfume (for the heroine).

Like the film, Smell-O-Vision was a commercial and critical flop.

The Caminito deteriorated in the following years, and became known as the most dangerous walkway in the world. After a series of deaths, the entrances were sealed up in 2000.

Restoration work began in 2014, and the fully refurbished walkway was opened in March 2015.

From start to finish it is 7.7 km long, but it is a walk rather than a hike, without ascents or descents, and it takes most people between two and three hours. It is a linear course, not circular, and your ticket includes a bus transfer back to where you started.

This is Andalusia – do we even need to say that the drive to the start point is spectacular? Driving around the Conde de Guadalhorce reservoir presents glimpses of lagoon green waters through the pine trees. Travelling south off the A-7286 past the Mirador de Tres Embalses, you can enjoy views of the impressive infrastructure surrounding this hydroelectric installation.

If the car park is full you leave your car clinging precariously to the embankment over the reservoir, and then walk back down the road that accesses the tunnel entry to the Caminito. Entering from the bright Spanish sun, it is Kapoor black in the tunnel, so have your phone torch at the ready!

Most photos of the Caminito depict the dramatic, high-sided canyon with river below, and a puny, filigree path suspended improbably about a third of the way up the vertical rock face.

Don't worry, there is plenty of this iconic experience to be had, but the first stages of the walk are through majestic valley scenery that betrays no hint of the rocky funnel ahead.

The new Caminito is solidly constructed, and feels very safe, although if you get severe attacks of vertigo you might want to give it a miss. Which would be a shame: it is one of those rare occasions when the word "spectacular" is thoroughly deserved.

The bus journey back to the car might involve a bit of a wait. In our case there was also some confusion over tickets, but as is the usually the case in Spain, good-natured negotiation resolved the problem.

Back at the car parking area, there are a number of bars and restaurants along the road with good views over the reservoir, so you can finish up with a decent dinner served on a balcony, nicely up and out of the way of the cars and the walkers.

History

Al-Andalus

Andalusía – and indeed most of Spain – was under Muslim rule for nearly 800 years, from 711 to 1492. This is longer than the country's 500-year Roman period, and longer than its Christian period, which is 529 years at the time of writing.

This Muslim period is fascinating, but many people are put off learning about it because it is so confusing. And who can blame them? If you haven't grown up hearing about the Abassids, the Almoravids, the Almohads, Averroes and Abd Al-Rahman, they can seem like a bewildering cacophany. And how on earth does El Cid fit into it all?

Fear not, there is a handy short-cut. It involves a bit of over-simplification, but the history of Al-Andalus can be divided into four distinct periods:

1. The Ummayads, from 711

2. The 30 mini-states, from 1030

3. The Fundamentalists, from 1092

4. Granada, from 1237

Armed with this simplifying structure, let's see if we can make some sense of Al-Andalus' remarkable story.

The first thing to understand is that Al-Andalus is not the same as Andalusía. Al-Andalus is the name for the area under Muslim rule during this period. It included almost all of the Iberian Peninsula, and for a time southern France as well. It was established by Muslim invaders, predominantly Arabs from Syria and Berbers from North Africa.

The word "Moor" is confusing: it was used by Christians to denote anyone living in Al-Andalus and North Africa who was Muslim. The great majority of Muslims in of Al-Andalus were not invaders or immigrants from North Africa: they were people of Iberian origin whose families had converted to Islam over the centuries.

Today, Andalusía is the southernmost autonomous region of Spain. The word was originally an adjective derived from Al-Andalus. Andalusía gained its current geographical shape when the Christian reconquista was completed in 1492, but it only became a formal autonomous region within the country of Spain in 1982. Andalucía is the Spanish spelling and Andalusia is the anglicised version.

Al-Andalus is usually said to have been named after the Vandals, which is odd, since they ruled the area only fleetingly, in the fifth century. When the Roman empire collapsed in the mid-fifth century, the people who replaced them for 300 years were the Visigoths.

They were weakened by squabbles between rivals for the crown, and in 711, the Moorish commander Tariq ibn-Ziyad crossed the 15-mile stretch of water to land at Gibraltar, which is named after him (Jebel Tariq – Tariq's hill). He went on to conquer the whole Visigothic kingdom in a seven-year campaign.

This is the story of what happened next.

1. The Ummayads, from 711 to 1030

The 319 years of Ummayad rule were the longest of our four periods, and the most successful in both geographic extent and cultural influence. The Ummayad capital was Cordoba, and at its peak it was Europe's most populous city, with a little under half a million inhabitants. The Ummayads were relatively tolerant rulers, and Muslims, Christians, and Jews lived side by side more peacefully than at any other time in Spanish history.

The most impressive phase of the Ummayad period began in 929, when Abd Al-Rahman III declared himself Caliph, the most senior figure in the Muslim world. There were paved streets and impressive public buildings, including the largest library in Europe. Scholars came to Al-Andalus from far and wide. The Caliph built himself a massive new fortified palace complex, the city of Medina Azahara, a few miles outside Cordoba.

Sadly this period of stability and cultural achievement was not sustained for long. Civil war broke out in 1009 and Cordoba was sacked in 1013. Two decades later, Al-Andalus disintegrated into a collection of petty kingdoms.

2. The 30 mini-states, from 1030 to 1092

The thirty or so mini-states which succeeded the Ummayads were called Taifas, from an Arabic word for faction. They were run by local strongmen, and they were always vulnerable to attack by the Christians in the north, and they were also vulnerable to each other. This situation was unstable, but it was also the natural state in the absence of a strong central ruling force: it re-emerged briefly on two later occasions when central regimes collapsed.

The most noteworthy character from this period was Rodrigo Díaz de Vivar, a mercenary known by the Moors as El Cid (lord), and by the Christians as El Campeador (master of the battlefield). A formidable mercenary general, he earned a reputation as an ideal medieval knight – strong, valiant, loyal, just, and pious. He fought for both Christians and Muslims, and towards the end of his life he became the ruler of an independent Valencia.

Under the Ummayads, the Christians to the north had paid tributes to the Muslims to avoid being raided or invaded. In the Taifa period this situation reversed, and eventually the beleaguered rulers appealed for help from across the Mediterranean. That proved to be a mistake.

3. The Fundamentalists, from 1092 to 1248

In 1086 the Taifas asked the Almoravid ruler of Morocco, Yusuf ibn Tashfin, to come and help them fend off Christian attacks. He succeeded, but four years later he returned and annexed the whole of Al-Andalus to the Almoravid empire, which stretched 2,000 miles from Zaragosa in the north to the south of what is now Mauritania.

The Almoravids probably got their name from an Arabic word for fortress, which is appropriate given their enthusiasm for the forcible conversion of unbelievers. They were Islamic fundamentalists who wore veils as a sign of their devotion to Allah, but their successors, the Almohads, were even more austere, and sneered that the veil was a sign of effeminacy.

Like the Almoravids, the Almohads were Berbers from North Africa. Their name denotes an insistence on the one-ness of Allah, and a rejection of perceived tendencies towards polytheism. After years of fighting, they took Marrakesh in 1147, and they quickly proceeded to take control of Al-Andalus too. They moved the capital to Seville, where they built the minaret of the great mosque, which now makes up most of the Giralda, the bell tower of Seville's cathedral.

Their reign was also short. They lost a decisive battle with the Christians in 1212, and in 1248 Seville fell. A year later, only the south-west corner of al-Andalus remained in Muslim hands. From then on, this remnant of Al-Andalus was living on borrowed time.

4. Granada, from 1237 to 1492

That borrowed time lasted for over 250 years. In 1237, the citizens of Granada invited Muhammad ibn Yusuf, a noted military commander, to become its ruler in the face of relentless Christian expansion. In 1246, Muhammad turned defeat into salvation by signing a treaty under which he paid substantial tribute to the Christian king of Castile and Leon in return for 20 years of peace.

This enabled him to consolidate his position and establish his dynasty, the Nasrids, which was maintained by making further payments, by playing the Christians off against each other, and by exploiting the geographical natural defences of their realm. It was Muhammad who built the first parts of the Alhambra fortress and palace.

The high point of Granada's time as the remaining part of Al-Andalus was the reign of Yusuf and his son Muhamad V in the 14th century. But there were plenty of low points too, with many of the Nasrids coming to power by murdering their relatives, and losing power the same way. Once the Christian kingdoms of Spain united, with the marriage of the king of Aragon and the queen of Castile, the fate of Granada was sealed. After some bloody battles (particularly the capture of Malaga) the Christians took most of the territory of the Kingdom of Granada. With the Christian army besieging the city, the Nasrids accepted their fate, and in 1492 the emir, Boabdil, handed over the keys to Granada without a fight.

Life in Al-Andalus

Around 80% of the population of Al-Andalus were Muladies – people of Iberian origin whose ancestors had converted to Islam. Above them in social status were Arabs from the

Below the Muladies were Mozarabes – people whose families had not converted to Islam from Christianity, but who spoke Arabic. Finally came the Jews. Under the Ummayads, all these groups were treated with respect. At other times, not so much.

During its phases of tolerance (celebrated in this monument in Seville), Al-Andalus was similar in some ways to ancient Greek culture. Like the Greeks, and unlike the Romans, for instance, it was tolerant of homosexuality. Moorish rulers often chose boys as their preferred sexual partners.

The Arabs introduced a wide variety of foodstuffs, spices and crops to Spain during the Al-Andalus period, including rice, cotton, sugarcane, oranges, lemons, apricots, spinach, carrots, and bananas.

The scientists and philosophers of al-Andalus, including Averroes, Avicenna, and Al-Zahrawi, were respected as scholars throughout Medieval Europe, and their work helped to inspire the Renaissance.

And of course, the legacy of al-Andalus includes some of the jewels of world architecture, including Cordoba's mosque, Seville's Giralda, and the Alhambra.

La Leyenda Negra – The Black Legend

Ever since the Middle Ages, Spain has received a lot of bad press. Its rulers have often been depicted as backward, cruel, and incompetent. Was there ever a more vicious institution than The Spanish Inquisition? Was there ever a more ignominious military reversal than the Spanish Armada of 1588? Did any other colonial power behave with such savagery as the Conquistadores in Peru and Mexico?

These charges were examined and rejected in "La Leyenda Negra" (The Black Legend), a book by a Spanish historian called Julián Juderías. It was published in 1914, and the question has been hotly debated ever since.

Criticism of Spain grew particularly intense in the 16th century when Protestant countries in Northern Europe confronted Philip II's militant Catholicism. One strand of the attack was the claim that the Spanish Inquisition was spectacularly harsh and cruel. In fact this was simply untrue: there were strict conditions about how and when the inquisitors could inflict torture, and they tried and executed far fewer people than other types of European courts had done throughout the Middle Ages. Ironically, one reason the Spanish Inquisition was established in 1478 was to fend off suspicions in the Vatican and elsewhere that Spain was overly tolerant of other religions, after 800 years of rule by Muslims.

For the English, the great set-piece battle with Spain was the Armada, Philip's attempted invasion in 1588. Philip was married to one of Henry VIII's daughters, known as Bloody Mary for her persecution of Protestants, and when she died, Philip regarded her successor Elizabeth I as an illegitimate heretic. He sent a fleet of 130 warships up the English Channel to team up with an army that was waiting in the Netherlands.

The story told in English schools is that the glamorous Sir Francis Drake displayed great composure, insisting on finishing his game of bowls before leading a fleet of small and nimble ships to a glorious naval victory against the incompetent Spaniards in their lumbering galleons.

The truth is that the English fleet, while inflicting some damage, was far less responsible for the Armada's failure than inclement weather. And although many Spanish ships were wrecked as they limped north around Scotland and south past Ireland, most of them returned safely home.

Furthermore, what relatively few English people know is that the following year, Drake led a counter-Armada, hoping to destroy the Spanish fleet as it underwent repairs in Spain, and seize the throne of Portugal.

This English Armada was no more successful than the Spanish one, with a third of the 150 ships lost.

Spain's status as Europe's superpower was extended for several more decades.

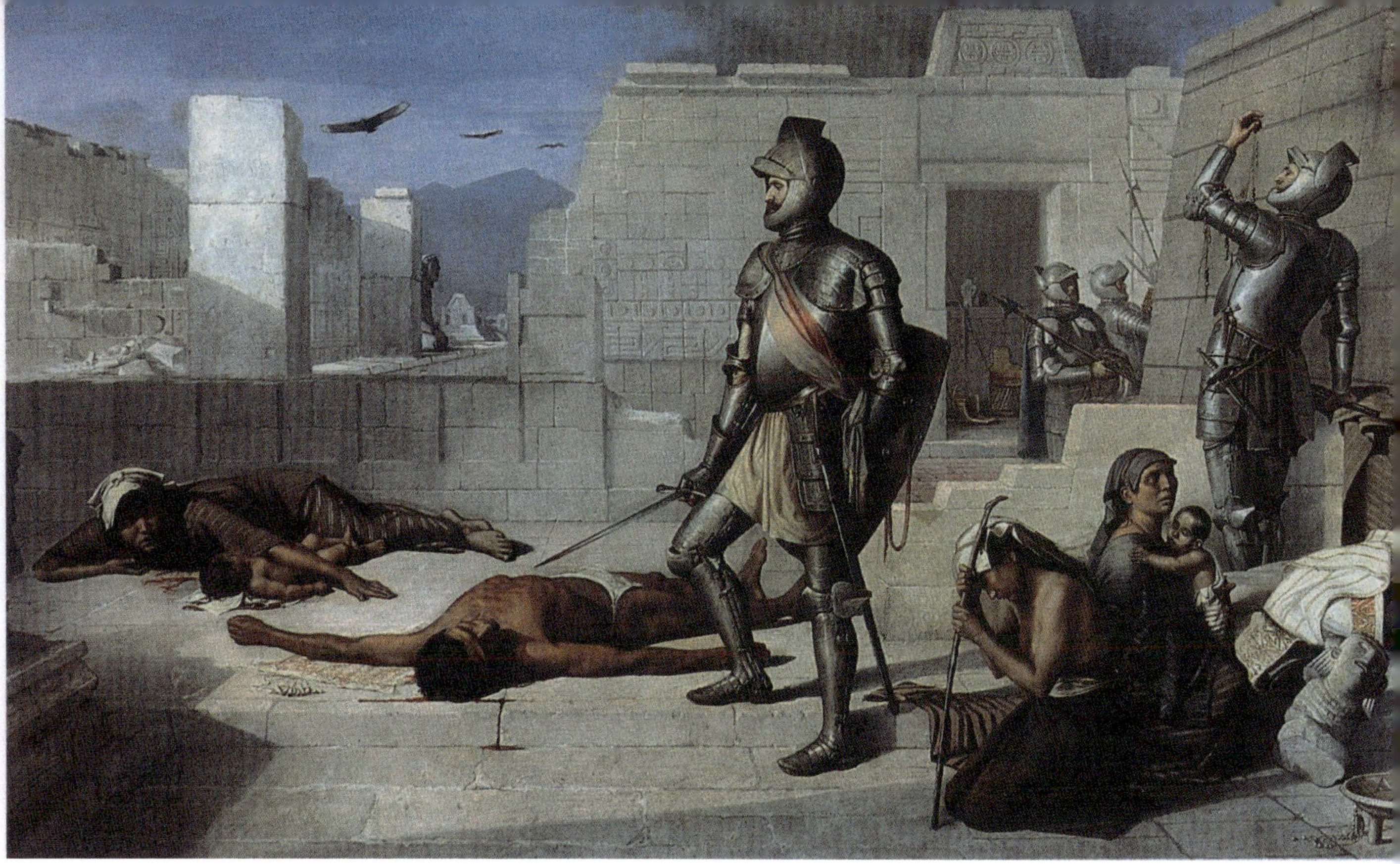

Another strand of the black legend is that Spain's colonisation of the Americas was especially vicious, and more damaging to the indigenous peoples than the empires of other European countries. As well as a naval commander, Drake had another career as a buccaneer, a kind of pirate licensed by his government to prey on ships flying the Spanish flag. This practice was justified in part by the claim that the Spanish were subjecting their Indian subjects to slavery.

The story of Spain's subjection of the Aztecs, the Maya, the Inca, and the other people they colonised in the Americas is indeed a brutal one. Hundred of thousands perished in fighting, and millions more died from the smallpox which the Spaniards imported unwittingly. Many of those who survived were effectively enslaved, and their cultures were systematically erased as idolatrous. Books and buildings were destroyed, and many fine artworks in gold and silver were melted down and turned into ingots and coins.

In an attempt to rebut the charge of exceptional cruelty, a so-called "white legend" was developed, which pointed out that slavery was formally prohibited in the Spanish colonies, and that priests like Bartolomé de las Casas campaigned against the savagery of the conquistadores. This revisionism goes too far, but it is fair to point out that other European colonial powers were no kinder or more altriustic than Spain.

The number of American Indians who perished during the colonisation of the USA and Canada remains disputed, but it was probably in the tens of millions. The forcible removal of entire Indian nations to what is now Oklahoma following the Indian removal Act of 1830 would probably be classed as a genocide if it happened today. Elsewhere, debate continues about whether the Black War of British colonialists against indigenous Tasmanians in 1825-32 was a systematic attempt at genocide, and the British are often said to have invented the concentration camp during the Boer War of 1899-1902. It is true that in 1833, the British became one of the first major nations to end slavery, but prior to that it had industrialised the institution, and slavery was the economic backbone of several of its major cities. Ironically, Sir Francis Drake was one of its pioneers.

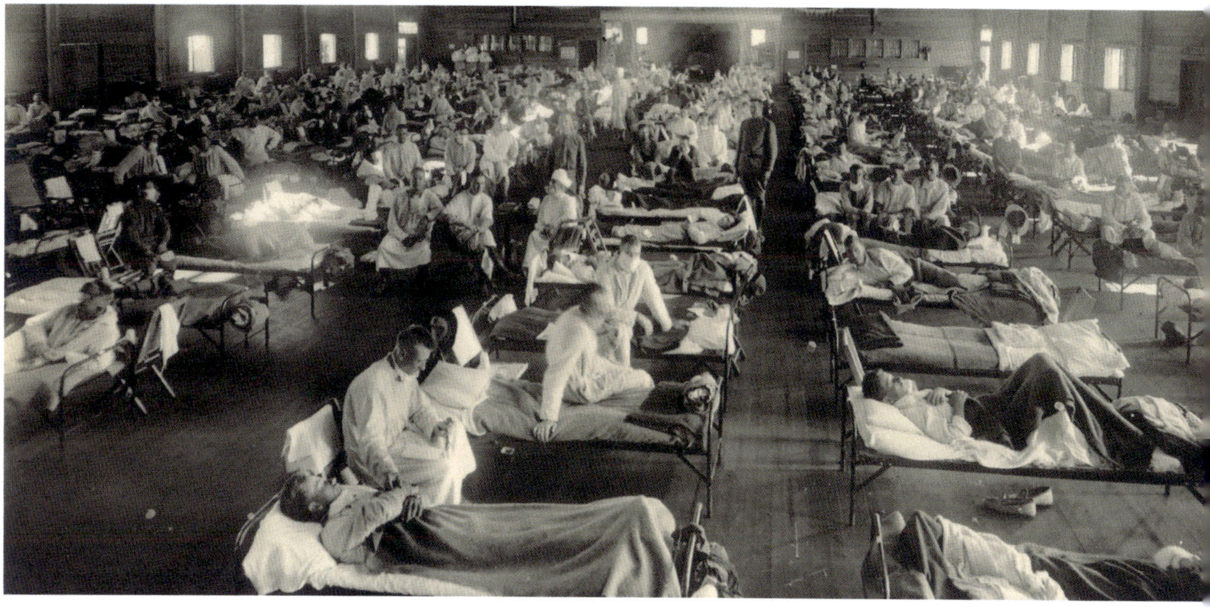

A final insult to Spanish pride has echoed since the arrival of the Covid pandemic in 2020. The terrible influenza epidemic of 1918-20 killed around 50 million people, more than the First World War which it followed. It has always been known as the Spanish flu, but it actually had nothing to do with Spain. As a non-combatant in the Great War, Spain imposed looser restrictions on its press. While neighbouring countries suppressed news of the carnage in order not to damage morale at a precarious time, the Spanish papers reported it openly. As a result, people assumed it was rampant in Spain long before its terrible impact was known about elsewhere.

Fortunately, none of these calumnies seem to bother the Spanish today. Spain is a magnificent country which has been a global superpower not once in its history, but twice. It lost that position long ago, and has reconciled itself completely to being at best a medium-sized player on the world stage. There are other countries which could learn a valuable lesson from that.

About

In 2016 we bought a house in Andalusia's Sierra de Ronda. The picture opposite is the view from its balcony, with Gibraltar in the distance, and the Rif mountains in Morocco visible across the Mediterranean. There are more pictures overleaf.

A couple of years later, we were browsing the internet, looking for an illustrated coffee-table book on the area as a lure to encourage a friend to visit. We were surprised not to find one we liked at a sensible price. So we decided to write one ourselves.

Book stores, online and offline, are awash with travel guides, and this is not one. Many travel guides are very good, but they are necessarily concise. Their writers have to cover a lot of ground, and they lack the freedom to expand on those aspects of a country's culture, architecture and landscape which interest them most. Travel guides are also pocket-sized, which reduces their scope for gorgeous pictures.

Travel writers, by contrast, spend months, and even years, researching the minutiae of a particular place or story, and conveying that in timeless prose.

This book is not trying to be as comprehensive as a travel guide, nor as lurid as literary travel writing.

Instead, it is intended to whet your appetite to visit a region that we love, and evoke fond memories if you have loved it too. It is a personal project, dictated solely by our own whims and fancies. We hope it will tickle yours.

We are both serial entrepreneurs. Calum is a writer and keynote speaker on the future of artificial intelligence. Julia offers online courses on interior design @recipe_for_a_room.

You can find us on Instagram at d1g1tal_n0mads.

The pictures opposite are from the house's page on Airbnb, which you can find by entering "Vista de Carmen, Gaucin" into Google.

List of photographs

Key to sources: A = authors, L = licensed, T = Turespana, C = creative commons
Our photos are "copyleft". You are welcome to use them under the Creative Commons CC BY-SA 4.0 license
Please let us know if we have mis-attributed any images. We will rectify in future editions

117	1812 Constitution Monument, Cadiz	L
118	Plaza, Cadiz	A
119	Gull, Cadiz	A
120	Gaucin castle seen from Vista de Carmen	A
122	Olvera	L
124	Gaucin seen from the Hacho mountain	A
125	Gaucin castle	A
126	Algatocin and Los Reales mountains	A
127	Gaucin street scene	A
128	Genalcgaucil	A
129	Gaucin seen from Vista de Carmen	A
130, 137	Zahara de la Sierra	L
131-136	Zahara de la Sierra	A
138-147	Juzcar	A
148-163	Hiking	A
164-173	Horses	L
174, 179, 180, 184	Caminito del Rey	L
177	Alfonso	L
178	Elizabeth Taylor	C
174-185	Caminito del Rey (other photos)	A
184	Carving at Alhambra	A
186	Alcazar, Seville	L
188	Statue of Abd ar Rahman	L
189	Cordoba mosque	A
190	Re-enactment in Oliva	C
191	Andalusian flag	C
191	Visigothic eagles	C
192	Mosque, Cordoba	L
194	Statue of El Cid at Burgos	C
196	Torre del Oro, Seville	T
198	Alhambra, Granada	L
200	Serving tea, Moorish style	L
201	Monument to Tolerance, Seville	L
202	Orange tree, Seville	A
203	Averroes	L
203	Avicenna	C
204	Spanish Inquisition	C
206	Spanish Inquisition by Goya	C
206	Philip II	C
207	Spanish Armada	C
208	Drake monument at Tavistock	C
208	Spanish Armada ship in stormy seas	L
209	The Massacre of Cholula by Felix Parra	C
210	British slavers	L
211	Emergency hospital in Kansas, 1919	C
212	View from Vista de Carmen	A
214	The authors	A
215	Vista de Carmen	A

Sources of creative commons photos:

14	Judicial districts of Andalucia	https://bit.ly/3vwh1FE
48	Patio del Yeso, Alcazar, Seville	https://bit.ly/3uvQs1V
114	Roman Theatre, Cadiz	https://bit.ly/3ftVXdi
115	Gran Teatro Falla, Cadiz	https://bit.ly/3yJe06X
116	Preparing to fight the English, Cadiz	https://bit.ly/34pUGgS
178	Elizabeth Taylor	https://bit.ly/3hpGsE1
190	Re-enactment in Oliva	https://bit.ly/3ut0DUT
191	Andalusian flag	https://bit.ly/3vHEmnG
191	Visigothic eagles	https://bit.ly/3vvYQ2F
194	Statue of El Cid at Burgos	https://bit.ly/2Uwej5l
203	Avicenna	https://bit.ly/2SCd3wJ
204	Spanish Inquisition	https://bit.ly/3yMwiUI
206	Spanish Inquisition by Goya	https://bit.ly/3fqCNF7
206	Philip II	https://bit.ly/3p1yUtG
207	Spanish Armada	https://bit.ly/3bZEtDE
208	Drake monument at Tavistock	https://bit.ly/3i05gmV
209	The Massacre of Cholula by Felix Parra	https://bit.ly/3fVGIZs
211	Emergency hospital in Kansas, 1919	https://bit.ly/2SAhlzh

Printed in Great Britain
by Amazon

23693293R00126